# RESERVOIR

# SAINT JULIAN PRESS

# POETRY

# RESERVOIR

Poems

by

Elaine Fletcher Chapman

Saint Julian Press
Houston

Published by
SAINT JULIAN PRESS, Inc.
2053 Cortlandt, Suite 200
Houston, Texas 77008

www.saintjulianpress.com

ISBN-13: 978-1-7330233-5-1
ISBN: 1-7330233-5-6
Library of Congress Control Number: 2020945554

Cover & Back Art Credit: Aliki Barnstone
Author Photo Credit: Robert M. Chapman, II

*For my beloved family, especially Jackson, Emma, & Caroline*

## SOLITARY ENDEAVOR

Yesterday on the reservoir, mid-day,

an egret flew beside me at eye level.

The herons kept to cool banks. When I turned

into the wind, I realized I had paddled

too far. Not the distance. Not the difficulty

of returning. But the lacking of reserves.

Seagulls in a line on the rail.

The sun bearing down.

# CONTENTS

In the Greening of the Reservoir / 1

The Invitation of *Hagia Sophia* / 2

In the Company of Friends / 3

Meditation on *Radiance Sutra #77* / 4

Lately, the Reservoir, My Ocean / 5

Spring Poem / 6

Three Days of Rain / 7

What We Need / 8

Urgency / 9

Present Landscape / 10

Under the Influence of Community / 11

Still Life at the Gathering Table / 12

We Remember Our Lives Governed by Moments
We Share with Loved Ones / 13

Returning to Merton in Winter / 14

Integrity / 15

Ars Poetica / 16

Lenten Psalm Relating to Snow / 17

Expectation / 18

Awakening to *Hagia Sophia* / 19

Love Poem to My Daughter on Turning Forty-Six / 20

Meditation on *Radiance Sutra #39*  /  21

Baking After Reading *Radiance Sutra #62*  /  23

Meditation on *Radiance Sutra #23*  /  24

Just This  /  25

Meditation on *Radiance Sutra #25*  /  26

October Thursday  /  27

Meditation on *Radiance Sutra #37*  /  28

Meditation on *Radiance Sutra #98*  /  29

Meditation on *Radiance Sutra #100*  /  30

Channeling *Hagia Sophia*  /  31

The Month Passes Quickly  /  32

The Truth of Imagination  /  33

Afternoon at the Parsonage  /  34

Sabbath  /  35

Object Lessons  /  36

Virginia, Early January  /  37

Women in the Family  /  38

Writing  /  39

Meditation on *Radiance Sutra #81*  /  40

March  /  41

Unto Myself: Rejoice  /  42

Watering the Plants,
I Meditated on the Funeral This Afternoon   /   43

On the Topic of Empathy   /   44

Morning Meditation   /   45

Fall Haiku   /   46

After Driving Through Two Major Storms,
We Arrive Exhausted on the Outer Banks of North Carolina   /   47

Mediation on *Radiance Sutra #74*   /   48

Walking the Beach   /   49

*I Am the Utter Poverty of God*   /   50

Follow the Instructions   /   51

Reservoir: A Cycle of Haiku   /   52

We Know Little About Where We Come From   /   57

The Night Face of *Hagia Sophia*   /   58

Early May, Mid-Morning   /   59

*If we do not see what is in our reservoir, we will understand all new things in the same old-patterned way— and nothing new will ever happen... Contemplation actually fills our reservoir with clear, clean water that allows us to encounter experience free of old patterns.*

Richard Rohr, *Just This*

*There is in all things an inexhaustible sweetness and purity, a silence that is a fount of action and joy. It rises up in wordless gentleness and flows out to me from the unseen roots of all created being, welcoming me tenderly, saluting me with indescribable humility.*

Thomas Merton, *Hagia Sophia*

*Love calls our attention and engages us... Life as a mysterious self-renewing process.*

*The Radiance Sutras*, translated by Lorin Roche, PhD

# RESERVOIR

# IN THE GREENING OF THE RESERVOIR

In a few short weeks we lose
the long view. At the same time,
the large dogwood moves in close.
Even in pre–dawn, the brilliant
white casts light into the second–floor kitchen:
*tree level.* Eye to eye with blossoms.
Our house, a *split level.* And below the pink
and purple azaleas, winter pot of pansies.
The red, yellow, and green prayer flags
tied between trees.

Next Monday our *gathering* table
arrives. Old pine boards with knots
and even a burn mark. Weathered. A dark
finish. Used well for over a hundred years.
Until now, I always felt round best.
This new one, long, like commitment.
An anniversary vow seeing anew.
A greeting of possibilities found
in the changing of seasons
and an old farm table.

# THE INVITATION OF *HAGIA SOPHIA*

She created her own labyrinth,

walking the perimeter of the church

yard several times a day: Circle Walking.

She began picking up litter: a child's glove,

an empty beer can, candy wrappers. Yesterday

she found an aged rabbit skull.


Accept what is given. Today the chill lifted

and the swamp beside the reservoir smelled

ripe with thaw. She noticed several trees

at the point taken by water. Her tribe

is scattered and she cannot gather them.

The sun offers radiance and mercy,

humility, *hiddenness.*

# IN THE COMPANY OF FRIENDS

Turtles laid eggs in the back yard
the week we moved in.
A good omen, turtles.
Summer foliage keeps the reservoir distant.
No salt, no tide.
A light rain and gray sky.
And an owl lives close by.
We live on the west side now.

The mouth of the York River,
a twenty minute drive down a dismal
highway. I will never give up
longing for the ocean.
Even with a measure of divinity and dirt.
The lovely slope, and vines. A bench.
The blessed angel under the dogwood.
What evidence of turtles now?
Any day, the pull again toward shore.

## RADIANCE SUTRA #77

*The heart of the universe pulses in all hearts.*
*There is One who is the life in all forms.*
*There is One who is joyful in simple existing——*
   *In all bodies,*
   *As all bodies.*

*Explore the life that is the life of your present form.*
*One day you will discover*
*It is not different*
*From the life of the Secret One,*
*And your heart will sing triumphant songs*
*Of being at home everywhere.*
translated by Lorin Roche

## MEDITATION ON *RADIANCE SUTRA #77*

I close the blinds to traffic on Harpersville,
trash people threw last night while passing.
Later I will pick up plastic cups and wrappers
from Sonic and McDonalds. Cigarette butts.

I open the blinds facing the reservoir, morning
light through the newly budding leaves. Some
call it scrub brush. I call it forest, the woods.

We take what is offered. Attempt to make
it our own. We are *temporary*. The parsonage:
Not a borrowed house, but an earned one.
When the choir director lived here, the living room
housed his practice organ. Walls hold
vibrations. Yesterday, when waking from a deep sleep,
I heard the chords from a chorus of soft *Amens*.

## LATELY, THE RESERVOIR, MY OCEAN


This morning I baked blueberry scones,
added leftover slivers of black pepper
cheese to eggs along with a slice of mozzarella, a little cream.

From the kitchen table in winter we see clearly
the tideless body of water. A steady downpour.
The birds, taking cover, disappear.
We depend on them so.

My beloved, on the phone planning a funeral
for an elderly man who died yesterday afternoon.
With each death, my husband misses his daughter
more. His only one. Nearly a decade ago

she sided with her mother. I like to think
she didn't have a choice. Still, she has yet to return.
Yesterday he preached the Transfiguration story.
Coming down from the mountain
always difficult. That fall from Grace.

Almost mid–morning.
Finally, I see two egrets crisscrossing. Butter and jam
still on the table. Tea, cold. Alone now. Years earlier
I prayed for solitude. Before the reservoir.

## SPRING POEM

It's a common story: finding one's way back.

Woolf wrote, *some closing of a chapter and peace*

*that comes with it.* In preparation for beginning anew,

and April approaching, with renewed promise.

Last week we discovered the afternoon light

in this house, honey colored.


We're invested in the unlikely calmness of the season.

Lent lending itself to the rare sighting three days ago.

An eagle gliding across the reservoir. Not soaring.

I believe in omens, opening a book to a random page.

Guidance and prediction. A new folder on the desk.

Today, perhaps the last spring frost.

# THREE DAYS OF RAIN

Another hurricane offshore,
another shooting yesterday
all but ordinary.

Opened the front door and removed the mail.
Only one piece today, a catalogue.
Turbulence in the Atlantic. East coast shorelines

bracing for erosion. Flood warnings and school closings,
perhaps for weather, perhaps for safety.
Five inches of rain are expected.

Poquoson already flooded and the marina
on Wormly Creek hauling boats from the water.

## WHAT WE NEED
### for Josh


I embrace the cool wind
and clarity of mind,
watching for egrets in the marsh
like Thoreau in his swamp.

Later before bed,
long after sunset,
while listening for geese,
a last call came, searching
for recognition and unconditional
love in a cruel, unjust world
where it is difficult to locate
the Divine on the long commute
home from the city.

## URGENCY

Last night I talked my son through the city; over the Golden Gate,
past Sausalito, to San Anselmo while my husband drove
to a hospital and sat with a man who discovered his wife
on the bathroom floor. Hemorrhage to the brain. Passing
from one world to another. And this morning I watered
the plants while he drove back to anoint her with oil and pray.
No children. Only a nephew and a ninety–year–old uncle.
It was a restless night. No one understands my urgency.

A few hours ago, I watched two herons circle high overhead.
We must love fiercely. We must say, *open your eyes. Look at me.*
It is midsummer. And the heat, oppressive. Some days it is hard
to breathe. Last night I woke in a sweat, even my hair, wet.
Too many days have passed since I looked my loved ones
in the eyes. I hear their voices. I render myself helpless.
And my husband's daughter, still estranged. No plan
for reconciliation. The woman's ventilator removed an hour ago.
She is breathing on her own. Her dying may take several days.
And we prepare for yet another funeral. We say, *I love you.*
We say, *we will be together soon.*

# PRESENT LANDSCAPE

From our house there is no safe place
to walk or ride a bike.
A stray bullet from the interstate
hit a window of a shop nearby.
There are no sidewalks.
We don't go to the nearest grocery alone
after dark. The sign on the backyard
chain link fence says *U.S. Government Property.*
We can't access the reservoir on foot.
Our side yard, the church parking lot.
And last week an electric sign that changes colors
with its message. We closed the blinds.

This time not exile. But hostage.
If we stay inside too long, we forget
we can drive away.

# UNDER THE INFLUENCE OF COMMUNITY

There is a measure we can't wait to measure.
Everyone guards his or her own wound.
Birdsong waits my awakening. And acceptance
comes with the greening of Vermont, the summer solstice.
Call and response. Healing, whole, holy.
And Kevin Young says *Amen* in the Carriage Barn
and we believe him. And two more Amens.
We don't hold back our appreciation
of the unmowed meadows. Again: Amen, Amen.

# STILL LIFE AT THE GATHERING TABLE

I raised the blind this morning
and discovered fog on the reservoir,
the swollen banks nearly in the backyard.

Not high tide but rainfall.
Bare branches fallen in the last storm.
Alone in the house for several days.

My husband at Holy Cross in Berryville,
me walking room to room turning off lights
left on all night.

The temperature still freezing.
Sit by the kitchen window,
watch for birds: a cardinal, highflying hawk.

Across the reservoir, a few egrets, still.
Geese floating, maybe six or so. I can't see
clearly. And now the red–breasted robin

under the dogwood. In my notebook I wrote,
*in medias res.* I say, begin in the middle.
Sometimes I say, start at the beginning.

The fog lifting. A few more robins.
I wrote, *not getting away but moving inward.*
My other hand, resting on the bare table.

## WE REMEMBER OUR LIVES GOVERENED BY MOMENTS WE SHARE WITH LOVED ONES

The dog barks when we kiss.
So we sneak around so he doesn't hear us.
He knows the sound of our lips touching.
A hug before sunrise, before we open the shades.
Unexpectedly, he sleeps at the end of the bed.

# RETURNING TO MERTON IN WINTER

There is in all visible things an invisible fecundity,
a dimmed light, a meek namelessness, a hidden wholeness.
Thomas Merton, *Hagia Sophia*

Early morning and a layer of frost
covering the grass, pine needles and cones.
The short morning walk. The hard earth.
The reservoir, a thin layer of ice,
starting at the shoreline. Geese calling
each other from a distance. One lone heron.

The work of the day begun.
Searching for what matters.
*You can make your life what you want.*
*Out of silence our Light has spoken.*
Our serious work, a meditation.

A teapot, a desk and chair, books.
A typewriter. Tending the fire.
A fallen tree and ferns. Stumps.
A stone wall imprinted with dead leaves.

Solitary behind the camera.
Perhaps momentary sullenness.
Peeling paint, weeds, an empty wooden bowl
beside an empty chair.
A cold day and bare branches overhead.

# INTEGRITY

All week the city's homeless stayed next door.
I didn't make brownies, peel carrots,
serve lunch, dinner, or breakfast. Instead, I watched
nightly from my kitchen window as people poured
from the door to smoke. I have nothing
to give. Not even a friendly gesture, no encouraging
words. After forty years of *helping*. One person or family
at a time. I could not walk across the parking lot. Make that journey.
Last year it was the same. Now, they are gone. Moved
to another church, in another part of town. At least for the cold
months. A relief, not to feel judged. *Preacher's wife*.
A relief, not to feel shame I place on myself.

## ARS POETICA

The stillness of winter
caught between
the small birds
stirring fallen leaves.
A small deer herd
hugging the wire fence.
The sun slow
at rising, bands of light
repeating pink.
The eagles' nest empty.
It's like walking the beach
until you find a treasure.
You know it when you see it,
bring it home, place it on a shelf,
or press it in a book to rediscover later.
In this place it's the sightings.
Walk until a *vision* appears
or someone pulls into the adjacent
parking lot and distracts you
from your mission of imagining
you are in a far removed
wilderness, solitary.

## LENTEN PSALM RELATING TO SNOW

We're huddled in the house.
Even the dog is under a blanket.
And I'm trying to let go
of the past. I hear
*pray with humble madness.*
I'm on my knees
while my husband sorts
papers in the living room:
old bulletins, funeral programs,
orders of worship, unopened
Christmas cards.

This morning we forgot
our daily devotion.
Is it too late?
Now, cold temperatures
cancel our plans.
The day—old soup simmers
on the stove. We ate all
the cheese yesterday.
Can I not lose faith?
The wind remains strong.
Snow blows everywhere.
I hear the wind chimes
from the front porch
breaking the silence
while I wait.

# EXPECTATION

Outside I looked
for carnage,
there was none
that I could see.
No sign from the night,
nothing amiss.
We rarely look up
at the night sky.
Stars dimmed
by so much light.
Searching
for any change,
or perhaps a sign
of significance,
a message from *Sophia*.
I wonder how the heron
stands in the cold water
for such a long time,
waiting.

## AWAKENING TO *HAGIA SOPHIA*

It is not enough to wake to a full moon,
wake to a subtle memory
of the comfort a stand of trees provided.
This staring started early,
anticipating an arrival or rescue.
A vigil. Waiting for a likeness,
a sound, a signal. All along
following a singular thread.
Studying xylem and phloem.
The chemistry of leaves,
cleansing breath. Breathing in unison.
The body breathing itself.
The anthropology of roots,
seeds. It's winter.
Gum balls and red magnolia seeds.
Elms in this backyard
alongside the old dogwood.

# LOVE POEM TO MY DAUGHTER
## ON TURNING FORTY–SIX

*for Alex*


Vow to do what matters:
Love hard, yourself
as well as others.
Take to heart your worth,
no matter what. Continue
to discover the unknown.
Be involved with weather.
Ride the ferry. Sit outside
in the wind. Get wet. Walk
briskly up Market Street.
During lunch walk down
to the museum. Find O'Keefe's
*Black Place I* then *Lake George*.
There will be an understanding.

RADIANCE SUTRA #39

*Cast aside the ten thousand things,*
*And love only one.*
*Don't go on to another.*

*Engage your lively awareness*
*With this one focus—*
*One object, one thought, one symbol.*
*Now go inside.*
*Find the center,*
*The soul, the heart.*

*Right here,*
*In the middle of the feeling,*
*Attend the blossoming——*
*Attention vast as the sky.*

translated by Lorin Roche

MEDITATION ON RADIANCE SUTRA #39

In the aftermath of renewal,
I'm left alone.

One red–headed woodpecker
in the woods off Noland Trail.
One osprey over Lake Maury.
One house sparrow in the backyard.

Nine days after Easter. A Tuesday.
Could be any Tuesday. We could say
distance doesn't matter. We could say
we are all one. We could say
separation is a myth. We could say
we are beyond space and time.

We hiked by the bay,
through the meadow
and down the winding path.
We sat on the bench and looked
over to the other side of the lake.

Afterwards she returned to Oakland.
I returned to my desk
to cast aside those *ten thousand things.*

*RADIANCE SUTRA #62*

*Enter the space inside your head.*
*See it as already infinite,*
*Extending forever in all directions.*

*This spaciousness that you are*
*Is permeated by luminosity.*
*Know this radiance*
*As the soul of the world.*
translated by Lorin Roche

## BAKING AFTER READING *RADIANCE SUTRA #62*

On Saturday making the Roman breakfast cake
was the closest I came to traveling.

The peak of egg whites, lemon
 zest infused sugar, the berries.

The recipe from someone's travel log.
What is it about acceptance?

The refusal to settle in.

For some reason
the fruit sank to the bottom.

I sliced the cake for the church brunch,
saving some behind for the next day.

## RADIANCE SUTRA #23

*Forget all of your ideas about the body—*
*It's this way or it's that way.*

*Just be with any area of it,*
*This present body,*
*As permeated with limitless space,*
*Drenched in freedom.*

translated by Lorin Roche

## MEDITATION ON *RADIANCE SUTRA #23*

All day yesterday I moved books,
placed them in alphabetical order, looked
for missing ones: Gilbert and Gregg.
And now I can't find *Gilead*.

Misplaced again. And the Merton journals.
My body aches. And the morning sun
has not yet hit the window beside my desk.
The dog asleep in the dining room.

Even so the blinds still closed, weary
from what we miss: tidal water, vigil.
My hair longer, the lilac ash faded
after a few weeks. Barefoot.

And Bishop's letters placed near
her poems. Then Gwendolyn Brooks before Bly.
A whole shelf for Woolf. Before breakfast,
a full body stretch, arms reaching to the sky.

## JUST THIS

"...the dawning of divine light in the stillness of our hearts."
Thomas Merton in a letter to Abdul Aziz


In the stillness of arctic air approaching
by this evening, I am alone for the first time
in days and only for a few hours.

Daylight dimmed by cloud covering.
This morning the eagle flew by so close,
broke off a leafless branch in mid–air.

So close I felt the air stir, and the sound
of the branch breaking, startling us
from behind. An omen, perhaps.

Entering liminal time, I picked the early daffodils
and brought them inside, before the deep freeze.

## RADIANCE SUTRA #25

*Attend to the skin*
*As a subtle boundary*
*Containing vastness.*

*Enter that pulsing immensity.*
*Discover that you are not separate*
*From anything there.*

*There is no inside,*
*There is no outside,*
*There is no other—*
*No object to meditate upon that is not you.*

translated by Lorin Roche

## MEDITATION ON *RADIANCE SUTRA #25*

By early afternoon she's exhausted
every option to redeem the morning,
never leaving the house. But still searching
for an opening… anywhere. She wanders
to the back window where flowering vines
and foliage block her view of the reservoir.

Some days it's what she hopes for: a glimpse
of an egret or the occasional heron. Rain
over the last several days have left her barren
of any view. Half—dressed, hair unbrushed.
Only one short call from San Francisco, conversation
in passing. Hearing briefly the chatter from *Philz*
*Coffee* on Front. Her longing for the *secret*
*ingredient* even stronger. It's not about her living,
but for this moment, her lacking: a familiar face, a city street.

## OCTOBER THURSDAY

We woke with the moon high,
the sun still below the horizon.

You put cream in my tea mistaking it for coffee,
laughed. Remembered yesterday we were sullen.

Humidity cleared after the night rain.
I'm looking for wilderness, anywhere.

My brother said the surf will be good tomorrow
so he left last night for the shore.

He lives with us part–time since he sold his house.
We added a chair to the kitchen table,

share our evening meals. Strange how families expand
and then contract. Yesterday, a discussion

about Rumi's *Gazing of the Beloved*. And this morning
at the field with the dog, we looked across to blazing leaves.

RADIANCE SUTRA #37

*Go to a wide—open space,*
*Gaze without looking anywhere.*

*The mind stops its building of thoughts,*
*And rests on its own foundation—*
*Immensity.*

*The light that you see by*
*Is the light that comes from inside.*
                                        translated by Lorin Roche


MEDITATION ON RADIANCE SUTRA #37


On the freeway to Williamsburg
they ripped up the trees
for another lane. Gone are the dogwoods.
The old growth. It was on the way
to the Muscarelle to see Botticelli's Venus
when I discovered the absence.
Entered through the glass doors, settled
on the Crucifixion. Venus on the wall
to the right. How is light born from wood?

I drove home through a dense rainstorm,
barely seeing the road.
And today the fifth Sunday in Lent.
Psalm 130. All desperation, a cry for help.
Botticelli's rendering of Divine.
*Gaze without looking anywhere.*
Suppose this morning the dogwood
in the side yard took flight.
And the white petals with their center crown
landed in the palm of your heart.

## RADIANCE SUTRA #98

*Be wildly devoted to someone, or something.*
*Cherish every perception.*
*At the same time, forget about control.*
*Allow the Beloved to be herself and to change.*

*Passion and compassion, holding and letting go——*
*This ache in your heart is holy.*
*Accept it as the rise of intimacy*
*With life's secret ways.*

*Devotion is the divine streaming through you*
*From that place in you before time.*
*Love's energy flows through your body,*
*Toward a body, and into eternity again.*
*Surrender to this current of devotion*
*And become one with the Body of Love.*

translated by Lorin Roche

## MEDITATION ON RADIANCE SUTRA #98
After Seeing Botticelli's *Madonna and Child*
(*Madonna of the Book*)

We begin in the dark,
the guides unknown.
We walk on stone floors,
moss, on fine white sand.
We know little. We watch
the tide, the morning sun,
stray clouds–drifting.
We imagine the moon.

We look into her face.
How He looks up.
Hands touching hands.
We find the one book.
The one verse, we repeat.
*Holy, Holy, Holy.*
Gold and lapis lazuli. Figs.
Cherries and candied oranges.

## RADIANCE SUTRA #100

*All this talk of purity and impurity,*
*These are just opinions. Beyond them*
*Are the miraculous energies of creation.*

*Rays of light from a trillion suns*
*Illumine the altar of your sky.*
*Rolling blue–green oceans*
*Sanctify the air you breathe.*
*In this moment, you are inhaling their blessing.*
*Who are you to call any of this pure or impure?*

*Find the center around which everything revolves——*
*Stand here and be flooded with joy.*
translated by Lorin Roche

## MEDITATION ON RADIANCE SUTRA #100

Today we return one last time to Botticelli.
Yesterday brown pelicans entered
the James, just downwind
from the shipyard.

Next week, we enter Holy week.

One crucifixion, one resurrection.

Potato salad, ham, deviled eggs
and baked beans. Bread pudding.

While the winter branches remain
scattered, the white azaleas
around the elm in full bloom.

## CHANNELING *HAGIA SOPHIA*

I stood under the pine,
looked straight up:
the eagle on a branch.
I swear he looked down,
flew across the reservoir.
I waited for him to return
then continued walking.
Yesterday I said to my husband:
*We have entered liminal*
*time.* We begin anew
in the middle of winter
with a half–moon high.
This morning, it's still true.
He prepares for church.
Then the eagle. On this day,
nothing appears the same.

# THE MONTH PASSES QUICKLY

The end of the month and groceries scarce:
grateful for eggs and apples.

Another church member died early this morning,
my husband with the family right now.

Yesterday he was called to the hospital
as we were leaving the house.

Later, he sent a message: *Go ahead
with your day.* And I did.

Clergy spouse. Preacher's wife.
I often think to myself:

Good that I have plenty of work.
Good that mostly I don't mind being alone.

# THE TRUTH OF IMAGINATION

Every morning no matter the weather,
the dog and I circle back behind the church,
focus on the reservoir, light breaking, the eagles' nest
in the tall pine. I've taken to carrying treats
in my coat pocket, allowing him to *go free*.
What happened to longing for a tide,
the sound of waves breaking?
Where and what is sacred, holy?
*The holiness of the Heart's affection.* Embrace
bewilderment. The pine cones underfoot. That heron
on the edge of the marsh. A fox's footprint in the mud.

# AFTERNOON AT THE PARSONAGE

The way my study is situated
on the southeast corner of the house
where only for a few hours
light does not directly enter
either window. On the opposite side,
we close the kitchen blinds before dusk
for privacy. Sometimes I almost forget
our proximity to the church.
The congregation makes
decisions by committee.
Last week they removed old shrubs
and planted new ones
in an orderly fashion. Took away
the randomness of *natural growth*.

# SABBATH

It's Communion Sunday.
The body and the blood,
twice in one day.
Yes, I receive the sacrament
twice in a matter of hours.
Say *Amen* twice. Swallow
the bread. Get on my knees,
pray. I know the liturgy
by heart. Do I feel changed?
Seldom. On occasion
tears come, unannounced.
Perhaps it's the hymn played.
Perhaps it's words spoken
softly, the gentle gaze
in the giving and receiving.
The one body.

OBJECT LESSONS

I opened the book, long forgotten
and found there an index card
where I recorded the number
of days in my monthly cycle,
marking the irregularities:
April, 23 days, May, 20 days. I noted
one period lasted 18 days
and began again after 31.
In the same book written on scrap paper:
*V.W. I don't believe in aging,*
*I believe in forever altering one's*
*aspect to the sun.*

This morning outside the kitchen,
a red–headed woodpecker.
Yesterday from my study,
a bald eagle at tree level.
It is difficult to make sense
of omission, disregard,
perhaps even disrespect, standing
firm in what I know and don't know.

In Vermont after 18 years, the term begins
without me. The temperature,
minus three. Snow covers the ground.
My heavy coat in the closet,
wool socks packed away.
Eliot's *Four Quartets* still
on the shelf. The familiar passage
unread at the appointed time.

I will record the days of this cycle:
a wolf moon last night,
a fullness of light
with snow in the Virginia forecast.
My aspect to the sun forever altered.

## VIRGINIA, EARLY JANUARY

With snow, the heroic reservoir frozen over.

Migrating birds no longer on the banks

or nearby branches. The brown marsh grasses,

white with crystals, bent at an angle.

A cruel north wind caught them unaware.

Morning and the dog confused,

his nose deep in snow. Our walk shortened.

The quiet, disturbing and beautiful.

## WOMEN IN THE FAMILY

We had a Bleeka, Serena, and a Ruth.
An Eleanor, Sara, Lillis, and Agnes.
A Helen and Helaine. A Becky. A Garnet.
And a Ruby. And Lizzie. And then Alana.

We have an Emma and a Caroline. A Kira
and a Kathleen. We have a Deborah, Marta,
and Alex. A Cindy and Marcella. A Gailey and Georgia.
Ginger, Erin and Carleigh. A Susie. An Alfreda and Oksana.

Alice. Olivia, Thaisa, Patricia. And now Lisa.
A Linda, Christine and a Jennifer. Another Carly
and a Carolyn and an Ella.  A Sherry and Kay.
Barbara and Nancy, Stephanie. And Elaine.

# WRITING

The din not blocked
but embraced.

Waiting
for the luxury of morning.

The particular solitude
of damp.

The lack of light.
Inquiry held.

Hair unbrushed.
Scar mid–cheek.

Deep circles under
the eyes. Unseen

circumstances.
Even celebration.

## RADIANCE SUTRA #81

*Drop the thought,*
*"I am this body,"*
*Abandon the limitation,*
*"I am only here in this specific place and time."*

*Embrace instead,*
*I am not my body.*
*I am not this place.*
*I am not this time.*
*There is no place.*
*There is no time.*

*Realize,*
*"I am everywhere,"*
*Sustained by infinite bliss.*
                    translated by Lorin Roche


## MEDITATION ON *RADIANCE SUTRA #81*


Perhaps if I could hear their voices,
feel the air from their breaths,
I could dismiss what's missing,
forget the body, forget time.

It's not only distance.
It's their lack
of desire that follows me
around the reservoir
this morning.

## MARCH

I forgot to include compassion.
Distracted by geese flying overhead.
I only heard them. Not knowing
if they were coming or going.
Perhaps heading north.
Homeward bound. I'm still asking,
*Where is home?* Our third spring here.
Not settled in or down. Temporary
as temperament, as timely.

I walk from room to room,
imagine what I will leave behind
when we move from this place.

## UNTO MYSELF: REJOICE

All falls away except the open field,
a shared omelet, the biscuit with apple butter.

The chilled Rose Cuvee for the evening meal.
Try not to recoil, hold any bitterness.

Not reconciliation but reconciling. Not descending
but ascending. The rainstorm passes quickly.

Cloud cover remains. I moved my desk
from facing the window and turned toward Matisse:

*Histoire Juives.* Away from houses and highway,
the congregation coming and going. Now when I look

the large elm appears in the window, framed. On another wall
I replaced *INSPIRE* with *WISH*. Summer ends

this week. No tears. Another attempt to place
my uncompromising wildness on yet another map.

## WATERING THE PLANTS THIS MORNING,
## I MEDITATE ON THE FUNERAL THIS AFTERNOON


A slight cloud cover has brought some relief
to the scorching temperatures. Insects eat the begonias
before they bloom. I ruled out a fall garden.
I'm beside myself once again with losses, others and mine.
It's continuous. This death march. This dying.
Today, at the funeral I'll read the dead woman's poem.
*Despair. Disappointment. Relief. The rain.* My husband will give
the Sermon of Resurrection. Everyone wants joy.
Her unexpected death. Buried today. We will gather
at the church, then graveside. Then the meal, afterwards.
Chicken salad. Baked pineapple. Fresh blueberry pie.
We'll come home exhausted. My husband's shirt under his robe,
soaked from sweat. We'll change our clothes in unison.
Sit at the kitchen table with cool water. In silence.
Then we'll take the dog for his walk.
Still in silence.

# ON THE TOPIC OF EMPATHY

Braided by cold air slipping under the door
and around the sills, I gather additional clothing:
wool socks, the sweater bought 15 years ago,
the one with the silver angel pinned to its neckline.
I'm in for the night. Snow began falling an hour
after ending our conversation about moving
to San Francisco. I've been trying to get back
since 1979 after reading John Muir and driving
to Pacific Grove alone with two small children
and two dogs in the red VW Bus. But now working in Vermont,
living in one small room. The shells I brought from North Carolina
line the bookcase. I secretly give them to those in need.
I write in my notebook: collect shells from Ocean Beach.
Yet another plan to conjoin one life with another.
Little patience left for division.
Rub my cold hands together, rings
slipping easily from my fingers. Cup them over my lips.
Blow gently a breath or two. Snow
banked against the window.

## MORNING MEDITATION

There is a single rose frozen in place,

beauty paralyzed. The gallant bloom

stands abandoned in the small side yard.

The sun barely up. I decline invisibility.

The difference between being present

and being presence. I take a vow.

Light the incense. *Pray with humble madness.*

## FALL HAIKU

Chilly in the house,
waking before the sunrise,
the dog warming me.

*

This morning, field wet
with dew, the sun rising late.
Layer of fog. Waiting.

*

Bright blue autumn sky,
his daughter's cruel unkindness.
Words caught in my throat.

## AFTER DRIVING THROUGH TWO MAJOR STORMS, WE ARRIVE EXHAUSTED ON THE OUTER BANKS OF NORTH CAROLINA

The sun streams on my face
blinding my right eye. I would close
the shade but this sun carries brightness
from the ocean. Rain droplets cover the doors
and deck, soaked from last night.
Deep pine woods surround this house
and I am home.

## RADIANCE SUTRA #74

*Radiant One, inquire:*
*Before desire arises in me, who am I?*
*Before I know anything, who am I?*

*Seek always the intimate joy*
*Of your original Self,*
*And move through this world in freedom.*

translated by Lorin Roche

## MEDITATION ON *RADIANCE SUTRA #74*

In a sermon last week my husband spoke about going home,
tasting water from his mother's kitchen facet.
Nazareth has but one spring.

When I was six, we moved from South Carolina.
The closest I come to returning home:
biting into a ripe peach and letting the juice
run from my mouth and fingers into dirt.

It's who I am: a child leaning over a backyard
porch in Columbia, eating a peach.

## WALKING THE BEACH

We arrived shortly after sunrise.
I say, *life depends on proximity*
*to an ocean.* Today, the Atlantic.
The waves smooth, folding one on top of the other.
Dark rain clouds in either direction.
The dog runs to catch sea foam. I take in the spray,
wade in warm water.  Once more, baptism.
*Remember your baptism*, my husband says before communion
each month. This sand. This ocean. This air. These companions.
My sacrament, my savior.

## I AM THE UTTER POVERTY OF GOD

*I am His emptiness, littleness, nothingness, lostness.*
Thomas Merton journal entry

She enters the day with birdsong,
a banquet. A quest for all that is left
undone, all that's missing.
Vacancy of spirit. A breach.
The eagle guarding her nest.
The egret high above, legs
tucked for flying. A cloudy day.
Cool for May. Always waiting
for an invitation, a welcoming.

# FOLLOW THE INSTRUCTIONS

Dragonflies flit back and forth over bushes in the front yard,
feeding off summer mosquitoes breeding in the marsh
behind the house. Early morning and already the temperature is 82.
It's July. Two shootings near us last night and my brother talks
about the gun he keeps in his car, locked. No one is safe.
And yesterday in San Francisco a young woman shot from behind
by a stranger. Random act, her boyfriend beside her. I'm searching
for the Divine's voice in this mess. Random, as well. For 17 days
people from the church brought us meals. Every day at 5.
And another arrived this week: clam chowder, crab biscuits,
and apple–cherry pie, homemade. Unannounced. Random.
Being fed. It's what we all want, healing and to be held. Safely held.

## RESERVOIR: CYCLE OF HAIKU

The Influence of Light

Still air before sun
rise because we know love alters
all things— being Presence

1

Before the trees leaf—
a few buds, a daffodil
a new resolve

2

You cannot hurry
the herons catching breakfast
leaving the shoreline

3


A stand of pines, trees
across the reservoir, all
the egrets– gone.


4


In a week leaves fill–
hinder the view, a glimmer
blue surface beyond


5


Clouds keep rolling in…
rain again in the forecast
the reservoir full

6

The mimosa tree
on the other side of the fence—
blossoms barely seen.

7

A powerful storm—
the aftermath of erosion
large dogwood bending

8

Rain again today
reservoir not visible
weeds growing wildly

9

Behold a sunburst
after many days of rain
vines and shining leaves

10

The angel watches
over the geraniums
Rainwater in shells

11

Disappeared behind
lush foliage, the reservoir
missing from our view

12

Such dark thunder clouds
toads and frogs are confused
thinking it is night

13

Squirrels eating berries
from the dogwood—a backyard
feast before autumn

14

As leaves fall away
the reservoir reappears—
deep sigh of relief.

# WE KNOW LITTLE ABOUT WHERE WE COME FROM

We know little about where we come from.
We begin with a melody locked inside
only to discover it was our mother's heart
beat. And for the rest of our lives
we enter every room
in search of the unheard, unseen.
The ceramic bowl broken for years.
Piecing the pattern together, holding
it until the glue sets.

I step back. Reenter
my body.  Always
in search of The Mother.
My own mother's love spent
before my birth & her death.
Our reservoir of salvation,
found in her repaired bowl.

## THE NIGHT FACE OF *HAGIA SOPHIA*

*It is like all minds coming back into awareness from all
distractions, cross–purposes and confusions, into unity of love.*
Thomas Merton, *Hagia Sophia*

This morning ten egrets stand
in the shallows nearest the house.
For the last five years
the reservoir has saved my life.
Last week for the first time
I found a red feather near
the outdoor sanctuary. It took
several days to trust its color.
I dread the coming
of spring when the vines
obscure the view. Just now
two green herons fly in tandem.
In the Gospel of Luke we are told
they left everything behind.
Go where you are called. Several nights
ago geese woke me from a deep sleep.
I listened for a long time. Stood at the back
window. Staring beyond the stand of elms.

## EARLY MAY, MID–MORNING

To write a poem is to say I am living
again. Opening the door to the known,
unknowing. Welcome and Hospitality.
The baby birds in the basket on the porch
disappeared. We want to believe they flew
away and live in the boxwood close by.
We stop and listen. Wait.

I stop mid–sentence, light the incense.
Beside myself with longing,
like the honeysuckle consuming the backyard,
like the prayer flags fallen to the ground.
Unrequited love. When it rains, a natural spring
runs along the tree line to the reservoir.
We cannot stop it nor do we want to change
the descending path. We welcome
shifting ground, erosion.  It suits us.
The subtle sand mixed with scattered leaves and soil.

# NOTES

**The Invitation of** *Hagia Sophia*, **Awakening to** *Hagia Sophia*, **Channeling** *Hagia Sophia* & **The Night Face of** *Hagia Sophia* were heavily influenced by the poem *Hagia Sophia* by Thomas Merton published in *Emblems of a Season of Fury* (New York: New Directions Paperback Original, 1961.) The discovery of Merton's poem and the companion texts by Christopher Pramuk: *At Play in Creation: Merton's Awakening to the Feminine Divine* (Collegeville, MN: Liturgical Press, 2015) and *Sophia: The Hidden Christ of Thomas Merton* (Collegeville, MN: Liturgical Press, 2009) were instrumental in the writing of these poems. The invitation was revealed and accepted.

*The Radiance Sutras: 112 Gateways To The Yoga Of Wonder & Delight* translated by Lorin Roche, PhD published by Sounds True in 2014 is a constant companion. The Sutras are the universal contemplative meditations of Vijnana Bhairava Tantra. It is said by Shiva Rea that "one of these sutras is enough to change a life." I found this to be true. In the midrash tradition, included are 10 poems as meditations on The Radiance Sutras: #77, #39, #62, #23, #25, #37, #98, #100, #81, and #74. Lorin Roche graciously gave me permission to include his translations in the text of this book. I am eternally grateful to him and his wife, Camille Maurine for the experience of embodying these meditations during retreat at Esalen Institute in Big Sur, California.

**Under the Influence of Community** is dedicated to Sven Birkerts and The Bennington Writing Seminars, Bennington College, Bennington, Vermont.

**Returning to Merton in Winter** is a contemplative study of *A Hidden Wholeness/The Visual World of Thomas Merton: Photographs by Thomas Merton and John Howard Griffin/Text by John Howard Griffin* published by Houghton Mifflin Company, 1970.

In **Expectation,** the line *a message from Sophia* is directly referencing Hagia Sophia-Wisdom, the Feminine Divine.

In **The Truth of Imagination** the title and line ...*The holiness of the Heart's affection* were written by John Keats in a letter to Benjamin Bailey on November 22, 1817: "O I wish I was as certain of the end of all your troubles as that momentary start about the authenticity of the Imagination. I am certain of nothing but the holiness of the Heart's affections and the truth of the Imagination." *Letters of Keats: A Selection Edited by Robert Gittings* published by Oxford University Press, 1970.

**Virginia, Early January** is influenced by and dedicated to Robert Bly.

The title of **Unto Myself: Rejoice** draws reference from Biblical texts.

In **Morning Meditation,** the line... *Pray with humble madness* was borrowed from an online course, "The Shadow" with Carolyn Myss and Andrew Harvey.

# ENDNOTE

The poems in this book were written before the 2020 Covid-19 Pandemic and worldwide Black Lives Matter marches and demonstrations for Racial Justice.

# ACKNOWLEDGMENTS

The author wishes to thank the editors of the journals in which these poems appeared:

*8 poems Journal:* "In the Greening of the Reservoir."

*Rabid Oak:* "Three Days of Rain," "Love Poem to My Daughter Turning Forty-Six," "Meditation on *Radiance Sutra #39.*"

*Hoot Review;* "We Remember Our Lives Governed By Moments We Share With Loved Ones. Far Too Few Minutes Spent In An Embrace."

*Cloudbank;* "Meditation on *Radiance Sutra #25.*"

*Amethyst Review: New Writing Engaging in the Sacred:* "Meditation on *Radiance Sutra #77,*" "Expectation."

# FURTHER ACKNOWLEDGEMENTS

I am forever grateful to my parents, Charles Dorsey Walters, II and Eleanor Rue Fletcher Walters for permitting me to spend hours in libraries and allowing me to read undisturbed by my four brothers: Karl, Tim, Gary, and Wayne. Reading afforded me privacy, and a sense that I was participating in a sacred act. Early on, I noticed my father writing notes in a composition book. Unknowingly, his notetaking gave me permission to keep my own short notes. Later, I called these notes poems.

I have been blessed with extraordinary teachers whose guidance and wisdom remain present in my everyday: the late Liam Rector, Lucie Brock-Broido, and Jason Shinder. Also, Sven Birkerts, Janet Sylvester, Scott Cairns, Richard Miller, Alice Mattison, Ed Ochester, Stephanie Lopez, Clearlight Gerald, and Melisine Alegre. Their teachings and voices are ever present.

I owe a great debt for the kindness of dear friends: Tracy Rice Weber, Wyn Cooper, and Stephen Page who spent time with this manuscript, Catherine Parnell, JoeAnn Hart, Camille Renshaw, Michael Hooker, Jen Bergmark, Robert V. Hansman, Victoria Whitaker Clausi, Janis Smith, and Jane Heiby. The Bennington Writing Seminars Alumni community continuously offers inspiration and kinship. And most recently I am deeply grateful to Suzanne Kingsbury and The Gateless Writers community for their unexpected enthusiastic love and support.

And thanks to the On Keeping a Journal group: Starla, Diana, Adrian, Merle and Jean. I am grateful for their loving support through the writing of these poems.

To the Chestnut Memorial United Methodist congregation of Newport News, Virginia, I owe deep gratitude for the grace of their beautiful parsonage on the reservoir.

A very special thank you and deep appreciation to my publisher, Ron Starbuck of Saint Julian Press for having faith in my work and for his vision, care, and generosity toward poets and poetry.

In deep appreciation to poet/visual artist, Aliki Barnstone for her magnificent watercolor used on the covers of this book.

Fate connected me with Laura Lipson and I am forever grateful. Her brilliance shines forth in everything she does. She created and produced poetry videos, along with the amazing video editor, Bob Grant. The collaboration between Laura, Bob and photographer Robert Chapman and myself was heart connected and joyful. I can never give enough thanks.

To H. Alex McFerron and Marta Smith McFerron, Joshua Ryan McFerron and Deb Wilder McFerron, Jackson Wilder McFerron, Emma Fletcher McFerron, and Caroline Gailey McFerron, I am eternally grateful for their love and presence in my life. Jackson, Emma and Caroline offer me infinite amounts of joy. Often Alex and Josh are my first and faithful readers.

Tim and Susie Walters have given me safe haven over many years. I offer deep gratitude for their generosity of sanctuary and solitude.

And finally, to my beloved husband, Robert M. Chapman, II whose deep understanding of the contemplative world encourages my soul every single day. I am eternally grateful for his love and tenderness in our day to day. He always keeps a candle lit for me in his heart.

# ABOUT THE AUTHOR

ELAINE FLETCHER CHAPMAN ~ (Formerly Elaine Walters McFerron) Author of *Hunger for Salt* (Saint Julian Press) and letterpress chapbook, *Double Solitude* (Green River Press). Her poems have appeared in: *Cloudbank, 8 poems Journal, Amethyst Review, The EcoTheo Review, Connotation, The Sun, Calyx, Poet Lore, Salamander* and others. She is an Associate Professor (Adjunct) of English at Old Dominion University in Virginia. She holds an MFA from Bennington Writing Seminars and worked on staff for 18 years. She founded The Writer's Studio, teaching poetry and nonfiction. A certified iRest® Yoga Nidra teacher, she offers Yoga Nidra Meditation and Yoga Nidra & Sacred Writing©. She also maintains a psychotherapy practice.

www.elainefletcherchapman.com

For Poetry Videos:
https:vimeo.com/elainefletcherchapman

CPSIA information can be obtained
at www.ICGtesting.com
Printed in the USA
FSHW021529210921
84914FS